BLS WORKING PAPERS

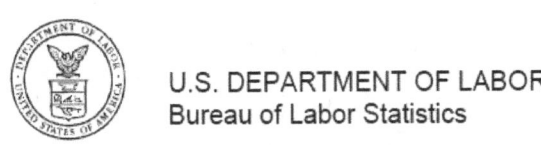 U.S. DEPARTMENT OF LABOR
Bureau of Labor Statistics

OFFICE OF PRICES AND LIVING
CONDITIONS

Quality Adjusted Indices for Four Year Colleges

Amy Ellen Schwartz, New York University
Benjamin P. Scafidi, Georgia State University

Working Paper 337
March 2001

The views expressed are those of the author and do not necessarily reflect the policies of the U.S. Bureau of Labor Statistics or the views of other staff members.   This paper was part of the U.S. Bureau of Labor Statistics Conference on *Issues in Measuring Price Change and Consumption* in Washington, DC, June 2000.

Quality Adjusted Price Indices for Four Year Colleges

Amy Ellen Schwartz
Wagner School of Public Service
New York University
Amy.schwartz@nyu.edu

Benjamin P. Scafidi
Andrew Young School of Policy Studies
Georgia State University
bscafidi@gsu.edu

Report Prepared for the Bureau of Labor Statistics

This work is funded under a contract with the Bureau of Labor Statistics (BLS). Any findings or views expressed in this paper are the authors' and do not necessarily represent the views of BLS. This work has benefited tremendously from the insight and advice of Dennis Fixler.

November 2000

Introduction

Since the earlier 1980's the "sticker price" or "list price" of a college education in the United States has, according to estimates from the Consumer Price Index, risen significantly faster than the overall rate of inflation. This has raised considerable concern among policymakers, parents and students that college attendance was becoming less and less affordable even as it was becoming more and more important for economic success in the job market. Interestingly, for the CPI, the government collects data on the "sticker price" of college (tuition and fees) without adjusting for scholarships given or other discounts. Further, no adjustments are made for changes in the quality or characteristics of the services provided, such as attributes of the faculty, the course offerings, or the facilities. Thus, the estimated price indices reflect changes in quality and characteristics of college as well as changes in prices.[1] In this paper, we develop and explore the construction of a quality-adjusted price index for US colleges, based on the estimation of a hedonic model of the price of college. Our focus is on estimating an index that reflects the out-of-pocket costs paid by a consumer in order to attend college and not, for example, an index of the cost of producing higher education services.

While many studies have considered the underlying causes of the growth in tuition, these have typically focused on investigating changes in the costs of higher education, the sources of revenues (especially government support and private contributions), or more generally on estimating aspects of the supply or demand for college education. There has been, to our

---

[1] For additional information, see "How BLS Measures Price Change in the Consumer Price Index for College Tuition and Fixed Fees" (1997).

1

knowledge, no previous work estimating quality-adjusted price indices and hedonic equations for college education.[2]

To estimate hedonic price models, we use data from the Annual Survey of Colleges (ASC) data from the College Board. These include data on financial aid and scholarships, characteristics of the student body (including test scores, demographics, enrollment), and attributes of the services provided by the college (including faculty characteristics, course offerings, athletics, etc.) We supplement the ASC data with data on tuition and fees from the Integrated Postsecondary Education Sata System (IPEDS) collected by the National Center for Education Statistics, U.S. Department of Education.

The purpose of this study is to identify quantifiable measures of quality of higher education services; to develop a methodology for quality-adjusting prices for changes in the attributes of college services; and to provide an empirical demonstration of the proposed method of quality adjustment.

The next section presents the theoretical and conceptual background for the empirical analysis including a simple economic model of college choice, and section III describes a hedonic model for estimation. Section IV contains a description of our data, and section V the estimates of the hedonic models. Conclusions are in section VI.

II.   The Market for College

The market for college education is characterized by discrete goods in which each contains a bundle of attributes valued by consumers, differentiated products, not-for-profit firms, imperfect competition, and heterogeneous consumers, among other 'familiar but curious'

---

[2] Articles by Charles T. Clotfelter and Gordon C. Winston and others in a Symposium on the Economics of Higher Education in the Winter 1999 Journal of Economic Perspectives pp. 3-116 provide a nice overview and introduction

idiosyncrasies which present formidable challenges to modeling supply and demand and understanding price determination.[3]   In this section, we review some of the most important features of the market for college that are relevant and important to motivating and understanding the hedonic analysis that forms the centerpiece of our method of estimating price indices below.

What do colleges produce?

While fully modeling the production process of a college is clearly outside the scope of this work, some discussion of the output of colleges is necessary. Colleges and universities are best viewed as multi-product firms, producing a variety of services including:

- Education
- Food, accommodations, and amusements
- Minor league "professional" athletics
- Research
- Investment management.[4]

Alternatively, Verry and Davies (1976) focus on the educational mission of colleges, listing outputs as follows:

"(i) *Instructional or teaching outputs* (the transmission of knowledge). This involves the teaching of various kinds (general, vocational etc.), in different subjects and at different levels, all generally leading to certification of some description.

(ii) *Research outputs* (the extension of knowledge).

(iii) *General Social Services.* This is something of a catch-all category for the less tangible and often most controversial activities of the university. It is intended to include the general socialization function (the instillation of desirable work habits, co-operative behaviour, respect for laws and institutions, and, some would say, docility and

---

to the field.
[3] See "The Familiar but Curious Economics of Higher Education: Introduction to a Symposium" by Charles Clotfelter (1999)
[4] This list is, in part, implicit in Ehrenberg (1999). Here, investment management refers to the management of the university's endowment and other financial resources. Minor league "professional" sports refers to high quality amateur sports where the athletes receive compensation in the form of scholarships in exchange for participation on an athletic team.

obedience), and the related function, primarily benefiting employers, of sorting, selecting and screening individuals…" (page 10.)

Understanding the objectives of universities is far from straightforward. Most universities are not-for-profit and might be viewed as acting to maximize some alternative objective function such as 'prestige,' 'human capital' or 'endowment' rather than profits. Universities compete with one another for the 'best' students – through the allocation of financial aid, the setting of tuition and the provision of attributes – in the face of resource constraints. Better students may enhance an institution's prestige/human capital/endowment by increasing the production of some of the outputs of college. Therefore, some of the customers of college—students—are inputs to the production process as well. (See Rothschild and White (1993) for more on this point.) For our purposes, the supply curve for the college attributes should be upward sloping – providing better attributes costs more and universities face capacity constraints that suggest increasing costs at some student body size.

What do students buy?

In paying for college, the consumer of undergraduate education buys only output (i). The college student (or her parents) is not buying research outputs (ii) or general social services (iii) directly with the price of tuition—the price of tuition does not entitle you to (ii) or (iii), which may be available to some other community. For example, research may enhance the prestige and/or learning experience at a particular college. These outputs are valued by various consumers that include, but are not limited to, college students. For example, university research is 'consumed' by governmental agencies and industrial clients far more frequently than by college students. The implication is that research, general social services and the 'other' outputs will be important in the hedonic analysis only to they extent they enhance the *undergraduate college experience*.

While universities produce many products, college admissions officers like to say that students (consumers) choose which college to attend based on "Resources and Reputation." That is, student choose a college based upon their perception of the reputation the school has (which may vary across regions for a particular school, for example) and the resources the school offers – such as language offerings, the availability of dormitories, or sororities, or the ratio of students to faculty. This suggests that in addition to including attributes that describe the resources provided by a college, a hedonic price equation should capture or control for the reputation of the college. 'Reputation effects' can be viewed as essentially the same as the 'brand effects' utilized in the hedonic analysis of automobiles or other goods. Our estimation strategy for the hedonic model described below allows for these brand effects.

More recently, some have argued that an additional and important output of a college is the increase in the student's future earnings or their 'market value,' often referred to as the 'value added' of the college. Thus, some would include a measure of 'value added' in the specification of the hedonic model. While calculations about the impact of a school on a child's future earnings is clearly an important consideration for students and parents choosing schools, it is unclear how those calculations are made given the available data. Put simply, we know of no broadly available data on the salaries of recent (or other) graduates or any other direct measure of the value-added to a student's education, for individual American colleges for the sample period of our analysis.[5]

---

[5] It seems that the relevant measures of value-added for a student considering enrolling in a particular college at time t would be the value-added to students who graduated at t-1. Presumably, prospective students would have better information about the value-added that individual schools provided to its recent graduates, than the value-added 4-5 years in the future. Recent research by Dale and Krueger (1999), however, has suggested that there are relatively

A model of consumer choice

This section describes a simple model of college choice, for a consumer who has already decided to attend a four-year college. (The choice of whether to go to college at all or whether to attend a two-year of four-year college is viewed as predetermined and therefore outside the model.) That is, we model a consumer's choice of a college, conditional on attendance at a four-year college.[6] The purpose of this exercise is to motivate the empirical model and to make clear the role that tuition and financial aid play in the college choice decision.

For our purposes, we view college as a discrete commodity with several attributes that contribute directly to consumer utility. Consumers cannot buy attributes directly and the prices of each individual attribute are not observed to the consumer. Instead, consumers can only buy attributes in bundles and the price of the bundle of attributes of college, the out-of-pocket tuition cost, is observed.

To be specific, assume that consumers value two attributes of college, X_{1j} and X_{2j}. X_{1j} and X_{2j} are observed by each consumer.[7] C_{ij} is the consumption of all other goods if student i attends college j, Y_i is household income, T_j is the sticker price of tuition at college j, and A_{ij} is the aid offered to student i at college j.[8] Let $U(X_{1j}, X_{2j}, C_{ij})$ be the utility that student i derives from attendance at college j. Student i chooses college j over college k if:

---

small differences in the earnings of students with similar characteristics due to the college that they attend. Thus, there may be smaller differences across colleges in the 'value-added' to student earnings than some suspect.

[6] Whether the student or her parents is the primary decision-maker will likely affect a household's willingness to pay for various attributes of college. Since this paper seeks to estimate the market value of those attributes and because the primary decision maker is unobserved, in the empirical work we assume that the average decision making power among students and their parents is unchanged over the sample period.

[7] In the empirical specification of the hedonic model in section III, some of the X's are observed and some are unobserved to the analysts. Since we have panel data, we allow for the presence of unobserved time invariant university attributes, "brand effects," in the hedonic model through a first differences specification.

[8] Rothschild and White (1996) suggest two reasons why colleges offer financial aid (A). 1) Given high fixed costs and low marginal costs, colleges can maximize net revenues through price discrimination. 2) Students can be viewed as inputs in the production of education. For colleges that offer aid to maximize net revenues, Rothschild and White believe that financial aid can be correctly viewed as a price discount. When financial aid is actually a payment to individual students for the inputs each provides, they believe that financial aid must be considered

(1) $\qquad U(X_{1j},X_{2j},C_{ij}) > U(X_{1k},X_{2k},C_{ik}), \ \forall \, k \neq j,$

where

(2) $\qquad C_{ij} = Y_i - (T_j - A_{ij})$ and $C_{ik} = Y_i - (T_k - A_{ik}).$

Substituting (2) into (1):

(3) $\qquad U(X_{1j},X_{2j}, Y_i - (T_j - A_{ij})) > U(X_{1k},X_{2k}, Y_i - (T_k - A_{ik})), \ \forall \, k \neq j,$

Each consumer observes its net price of sending its student to college j, $(T_j - A_{ij})$, but the prices of individual attributes of college are unobserved. Each consumer chooses which college to attend based on the bundle of attributes (the X's) that each college provides and the net price that she faces (T-A). Thus, from the consumer's point of view it is the *net price* and not the sticker or list price that matters for decision-making. Note that this implication is consistent with the empirical findings of Manski and Wise (1983). Their analysis of the postsecondary activity choices of 4000 students finds coefficients on tuition and financial aid that are almost equal and of opposite sign.[9] This suggests the net price should be used in the hedonic analysis and in the formation of price indices for the CPI.

---

differently. In our model, financial aid that is a payment for inputs provided by individual students may also be viewed as a price discount—from the consumer's point of view—if student inputs have a market value of zero outside of college. From her own point of view, an individual student's input is a sunk cost. Inputs provided by students can be viewed as their **presence** at the college providing excellence and/or diversity, each of which may provide positive peer effects in the production of education. In deciding which college to attend, consumers thus care about the excellence and diversity of their peers (and all other attributes of college) and their own net price of college—tuition minus aid. In our hedonic models described below, we include measures of excellence and diversity as attributes of college.

[9] Manski and Wise also include dormitory costs in their analysis and find similarly consistent results. "We might expect that a one-dollar increase in aid would have the same effect on a student's choice as a one-dollar decrease in cost. That is, other things equal, if tuition at school A is one dollar more than at school B, but if scholarship aid is one dollar more at school A than at school B, then a student should be indifferent between A and B. In fact, this is essentially what we find at four-year colleges and universities. The negative value associated with high tuition is almost identical to the negative value associated with dormitory cost, and each of these is approximately equal but opposite in sign to the positive value associated with scholarship aid." Page 19.

III. Hedonic Model

Estimating a quality-adjusted price index for college tuition proceeds with a hedonic analysis of the price of college based, conceptually, on the work in Rosen (1974) and following, essentially, the methodology outlined in Triplett (1990), Berndt (1991) and others.

Adopting a log-linear specification, the price of a year of school at the jth college at time t is written as a function of the characteristics of a year of college:

$$(4) \quad P_{jt} = \alpha + \beta_Z Z_j + \beta_X X_{jt} + \beta_S S_{jt} + \rho_t I_t + C_j + \varepsilon_{jt;} \qquad j=1,\ldots,J;\ t=1,\ldots,T.$$

where Z_j is a vector of time invariant characteristics of college j i.e., location, etc; X_{jt} is a vector of time varying characteristics of college j at time t, i.e., size of the undergraduate student body, student/faculty ratio, computers per students, availability of dorms, course offerings, religious affiliation, quality of the faculty; S_{jt} is a vector of time varying characteristics of the student body attending college j in time t, I_t are a vector of year dummies variables that take a value of one in year t for t=1,…, T; C_j is a dummy that takes on a value of one for college j (a college fixed, "brand," effect) and P_{jt} is the logarithm of the average price of a year at college j in time t.

Since few students actually pay the 'list' price for college because they receive at least some financial aid, we define P_{jt} as the 'net' or discounted price:

$$(5) \qquad\qquad\qquad P_{jt} = \ln(T_{jt} - A_{jt})$$

where T_{jt} is the tuition (plus fees) price for one year for one undergraduate student (full-time) at college j in time t, (the 'sticker price' or list price) and A_{jt} is average financial aid for one year at college j in time t. Financial aid was restricted to grants only—thus, student loans and work-study income were not included.[10] All public and institutional grants to students are included in the College Board's ASC data: Pell grants, other federal grants such as grants from the GI Bill, state merit and need-based grants, grants to students from institutions themselves, etc. Any private grants to students not reported to a university, such as an employer writing a check to an employee in order to offset a tuition payment for the employee's child, would not be included in the ASCs grants data.

As usual, equation (4) can be estimated to yield estimates of the marginal impacts of the characteristics of the colleges on their prices (βs). Each β is an estimate of the shadow price to consumers of a particular attribute of college. The coefficients ρ can be used to form a price index. Normalizing the level of the quality adjusted college price index to 100 in t, estimates of the price index for the following years can be created by exponentiating the ρ's. For example, the quality adjusted price index for $t + 1$ can be found as $100*\exp(\rho_{t+1})$; the quality adjusted price index for $t + 2$ can be found as $100*\exp(\rho_{t+2})$.

We estimate equation (4) in first differences, in order to purge the equation of the college fixed (brand) effects, which also eliminates the time-invariant variables Z_j from the equation. This has the added advantage of reducing any bias due to the omission of unobserved time-invariant characteristics. The disadvantage is that the coefficients are identified only by the variation across years. We estimate (4) using weighted least squares, where each observation is weighted by full-time equivalent enrollment in the first year of our sample to allow the estimates

---

[10] The College Board's ASC data include measures of average student loans and average income from work-study jobs. We did not include these variables in the financial aid measure. Ideally, we would include measures of the value of student loan terms and the value of work study jobs that are better than could be obtained in private capital or labor markets. If one of these forms of financial aid has increased (decreased) over time in terms of its scope and/or generosity, then our methodology will overstate (understate) increases in the net price of college.

to better reflect the actual distribution of spending in the market, as described in greater detail below.[11]

While the econometric strategy is relatively straightforward, estimation presents a host of conceptual and practical questions. In particular, what are the relevant characteristics that need to be included in the analysis? Are public and private colleges in the same market? To some extent, the answers depend upon the availability of data.

Note an important caveat about the price indices. The indices we estimate reflect only the change in net price of college services to students/consumers – and *not* the full set of services and outputs produced by colleges. Thus, since colleges are multi-product firms, we cannot use the price indices estimated in this paper to deflate total university expenditures to get a measure of university "output." For example, the benefits of research—an important university output valued by non-students—may be only partially capitalized in the net price of an undergraduate education. Obtaining measures of the value of all the outputs of a university and the full cost of providing those outputs is exceeding difficult (Winston 1999; Clotfelter, 1999) and is not the subject of this paper.

IV.   Data

We use five years of data from the College Board's Annual Survey of Colleges (ASC) for the academic years 1990-91 to 1994-95 and the National Center for Education Statistics' Integrated Postsecondary Education Data System (IPEDS) to estimate hedonic models following 1). The explanatory variables of a hedonic model of college should include only attributes of

---

[11] Note that fixing the weights used in the regression is analogous to fixing the quantity shares in the market basket used to create price indices. This weighting strategy, while providing a better measure of actual spending in the market relative to not weighting at all, leads to estimates of the upper bound of the actual changes in the price of

college that consumers value. This next subsection discusses the characteristics of college, and the subsection that follows describes our data.

The Characteristics of College

In principle, there is a long list of characteristics that would be necessary to fully describe the services (education; food, accommodations, and amusements; minor league professional athletics) provided by a college in exchange for a year's (discounted) tuition. These generally fall into four categories – characteristics of the instructional program and student body (peers), physical characteristics of the school and other non-academic amenities, institutional/organizational characteristics of the school, and the value-added to each student's human capital. We use a relatively parsimonious specification due, in large part, to the fixed effects specification which excludes all variables which are time-invariant either in principle or in practice – that is, some variables are excluded that could vary across time but are essentially unchanging in our sample and study period.

The Instructional Program. These include a broad range of characteristics and qualities of the instructional program - Average class size, number of seminars, course offerings (i.e., languages, labs, etc.), required (distribution) courses, pedagogical techniques, faculty characteristics (i.e., percent with Ph.D., percent with MA, number of Nobel prize winners?), percent of undergraduate courses taught by graduate students, publications of the faculty.

The Student Body. The characteristics of the study body include a broad range of potential variables describing the students' academic ability (i.e., average SAT scores, high school grades)

---

college. An alternative approach would be to update the weights annually, which would understate actual changes in the price of college. See Abraham, Greenlees, and Moulton (1998) for an explanation of this "substitution" issue.

11

and the students' socioeconomic backgrounds (race/ethnicity, age, sex), as well as their interests and abilities in non-academic areas.

School Characteristics – Physical Characteristics. These include physical characteristics (such as dorms or gyms) and environmental characteristics (i.e., location, climate, proximity to major city, or important amenities like beaches or ski slopes).

School Characteristics – Institutional Attributes. These should also include institutional characteristics such as their religious affiliation, accreditation, the presence of other schools, participation in an athletic conference, whether they are public or private colleges, and if public whether they are state or local colleges.

The Sample

The College Board's ASC data includes information on: (1) institutional aspects of colleges, for example, source of control (i.e., private vs. public), Carnegie classification, religious affiliation or accreditation; (2) environment (i.e, urban vs. rural) (3) facilities such as library holdings, availability of dorms (3) enrollment (part time, full time, etc.) (4) academic offerings and policies (5) fields of study (6) placement and credit policies (7) freshman admissions/profile (8) transfer study policies (9) Student life (sororities, intercollegiate sports, etc) and (10) Financial Aid.   Given the high rate of missing data on tuition and fees in the ASC data, we obtain the information on tuition and fees from IPEDS. Using the tuition & fees data from IPEDS increased our sample by approximately 100 colleges per year. Tables 1 and 2 provide data definitions and descriptive statistics for 1994-95 the variables that we include in our model. Although we estimate the empirical models with data from the years 1990-91 to 1994-

95, for ease of exposition, we report summary statistics for only the most recent year (table 2) and means for all years (table 3).

Our analysis sample includes only 4-year colleges that reported non-zero enrollment and expenditures with at least 20% of the student body undergraduates, following Winston (1999). In addition, they must have a Carnegie classification and must be located in the 50 U.S. states or Washington DC.[12] Like Winston, we exclude "Specialized Schools" as well; Appendix I describes these and the other Carnegie classifications.[13]

There are missing values for particular data elements in some observations. In addition observations may be missing for a particular school in a particular year for a variety of reasons. Most straightforward is that a college may have failed to return the data in a given year. Colleges have an incentive to provide data, since the College Board provides that data to high school seniors shopping for schools, however, that incentive may be more important for some schools than others.

Alternatively, a school may 'enter' or 'exit' because they fail to meet the criteria for inclusion in the sample – schools offering only a two-year degree in the early part of the study period may have offered a four year degree in the end, thus 'entering' the sample. Or, schools may have exited the 4-year market. This "entry" and "exit" is infrequent in terms of the number of students served by these schools. Given the missing data and entry and exit, we estimate the

---

[12] As described in the foreword of the 1994 Carnegie Foundation Report ,"the Carnegie Classification of Higher Education groups American colleges and universities according to their missions." All degree-granting colleges and universities in the United States that are accredited by an agency recognized by the U.S. Secretary of Education are classified in the following groups: Research Universities I, Research Universities II, Doctoral Universities I, Doctoral Universities II, Master's (Comprehensive) Universities and Colleges I, Master's (Comprehensive) Universities and Colleges II, Baccalaureate (Liberal Arts) Colleges I, Baccalaureate (Liberal Arts) Colleges II, Associate of Arts Colleges, Specialized Institutions. The groups are distinguished by the emphasis placed upon research, the degrees and courses of study offered and their admissions criteria, among others. See Appendix I for more information on these classifications.

[13] The Associates of Arts Colleges, which are also excluded from our analysis, typically do not graduate many (or any) students with bachelor's degrees, and the "Specialized School" are very small and very different in focus than the institutions included in our analysis.

hedonic model with a "balanced panel" of 534 colleges. Our 534-college sample differs from

this "unbalanced panel" of observations in the following ways. Our sample of colleges has, on

average, lower tuition, percent minority, average age of entering freshmen, part-time faculty, and

pupil-teacher ratio. In addition, our balanced panel has colleges that are much more likely to be

members of the NCAA or offer fraternities and sororities. Interestingly, the balanced panel is

very similar to the unbalanced panel in terms of SAT scores and number of students.

Table 2 also reports 1994-95 means for the two groups of colleges in our sample:

- *Graduate institutions.* Colleges that offer Ph.D. and/or Masters' degrees
  (Carnegie classifications Research I and II, Doctoral Universities I and II,
  Comprehensive Colleges I and II).

- *Undergraduate institutions.* Colleges that are purely undergraduate
  institutions (Carnegie classifications Liberal Arts I and II).

We split the sample in this manner because, as table 2 demonstrates, these institutions differ

greatly. Undergraduate institutions have a much higher mean sticker price than graduate

institutions, $13,572 to $6,190. In addition, undergraduate institutions tend to be much smaller

in size, have much smaller class sizes, fewer minority students, entering freshman with higher

verbal SAT scores, and are less likely to be members of the NCAA or have fraternities and

sororities.

Table 3 provides a time series of means for the variables used to estimate the hedonic

model. Although the sticker price of college, tuition plus fees, increased by 31.6% over the five

year period, the net price of college, tuition plus fees minus aid, increased by only 19% over

those five years.

V.   Results

Table 4 contains baseline regression results. As shown in specification (1) in table 4, an unweighted regression of the log of tuition and fees on the year dummies yields a monotonic annual increase in the "sticker" price of college. Weighting the regression by the number of FTE undergraduates in 1990-91, as done in specification (2) leads to a larger annual increase in the sticker price of college. Although a regression of the log of the net price of college [tuition plus fees minus aid—specification (3)] on the year dummies shows a monotonic annual increase, this rise in the net price of college is lower than the rise in the sticker price over the time period. As with the sticker price, weighting the regression of the log of the net price of college leads to a larger estimate of the annual increase in the net price of college. Specification (5) includes a dummy variable for purely undergraduate institutions, and the coefficient on this variable suggests that undergraduate institutions experienced slower net price increases over this time period, and the coefficient is statistically significant at the 1% level. Given this difference in the estimated net price inflation, we separate graduate and undergraduate institutions in specifications (6) and (7), and, again, the results show that net prices rose much slower in the undergraduate institutions. Given the possibility of substitution bias and the differences in the unweighted and weighted estimates, we believe that weighting the regressions is appropriate.

Table 5 contains the results of three weighted regressions of the log of net college price (tuition plus fees minus aid) on year dummies and several attributes of college. We present results for the full sample, graduate institutions, and undergraduate institutions, respectively. All variables are first differences in order to purge the regression of time-invariant "brand" effects and any omitted variable bias from unobserved and time-invariant attributes of college. Estimates of the coefficient on each attribute are interpreted as their shadow market prices. Note that the R^2 statistics from both the regressions estimated in first differences (the fixed effects estimator) are much lower than the R^2 statistics from ordinary least squares levels regressions (OLS) that do not purge the regressions of brand effects. [14] This is unsurprising since the fixed effects specification reflects only the time series variation while the levels specification reflects both time series and cross-sectional variation across colleges. An alternative method for estimating the fixed effects model explicitly includes a series of college-specific dummy variables and corresponding coefficients. The result is that the R^2 for the full sample regressions rises from .201 to .976, for the graduate institutions only rises from .208 to .972 and for undergraduate institutions from .208 to .969. The large increase in the R^2 reflects the substantial explanatory power of the college brand effects. The parameter estimates under this fixed effects specification are the same as those estimated in the first difference specification.

In the full sample results in table 5, most coefficients on the college attributes have the expected signs. Colleges with more part-time faculty and older entering freshman have lower net market prices, ceteris paribus.[15] Colleges that offer Ph.D. degrees, higher SAT scores of entering freshman, and a higher percentage of faculty with Ph.D. degrees have higher market net prices.[16] The brand effects were found to be jointly statistically significant. The estimates on the year dummy variables, the price index coefficients, are monotonically increasing over the sample

---

[14] As discussed previously, OLS in levels will yield biased estimates of the model parameters because of the presence of college "brand" effects.

[15] The model considers percent of students from racial and ethnic minorities, the average age of entering freshman, and standardized test scores of freshman as attributes of college that are valued by consumers of college. In the regressions reported in table 5, these three attributes are lagged. For example, the log of the net price charged for the 1993-94 academic year is a function of the percent of minority students enrolled in the 1992-93 academic year. Contemporaneous attributes of the student body (peers) may be correlated with the error term, and by using the lagged measures of these attributes we escape this problem. If marginal consumers truly choose which college to attend based on net prices and "resources and reputation," then the prior year measures are the measures of college quality on which they base their enrollment decisions.

[16] Some colleges reported SAT scores only, some reported ACT scores only, and some reported neither. To adjust for missing information on standardized test scores and the high correlation between SAT and ACT scores, we included an SAT score variable (75th percentile verbal score of the previous year's entering freshman) and two

period, but the estimated increase between 1992-93 and 1993-94 is very small. The sticker price

rise between those years was very low, 6%, while financial aid increased by an average of 20%.

We cannot point to one sweeping policy change regarding financial aid that caused the

substantial increase, but two small changes were contributors:

- A 12% rise in federal tuition aid to veterans (McPherson and Shapiro, 1998)

- The beginning of the state of Georgia's HOPE scholarship program, which offered free tuition and books at any Georgia public college to any Georgia high school graduate with a "B" average or better, and a substantial grant to eligible students attending a private college in the state (McPherson and Shapiro, 1998).

Based on the financial aid information reported in McPherson and Shapiro, the balance of the

rise in grants between 92-93 and 93-94 is likely due to state merit aid and grants from institutions

themselves.[17]

Regression results for the graduate and undergraduate institutions suggest that quality

adjusted price increases were much higher in the graduate institutions. Interestingly, the small

increase in net prices between 1992-93 and 1993-94 seems to be largely due to the lack of a net

price increase for undergraduate institutions. These regressions also reveal some differences in

the coefficients on the hedonic characteristics between graduate and undergraduate institutions.

These need to be interpreted with caution – differences may derive from differences in the

supply or demand factors determining prices in graduate and undergraduate institutions - and

disentangling these is beyond the scope of this paper.

Estimates from the seven baseline specifications in table 4 and three hedonic

specifications in table 5 are used to construct price indexes in table 6. These price indexes are

---

dummy variables. The first dummy equals one if the school reports and SAT score and is zero otherwise. The second equals one if SAT or ACT scores are required for admission.

[17] Based on tables in McPherson and Shapiro, we are able to rule out several programs as causes of the rise in aid between 92-93 and 93-94, Pell grants, state need-based aid, etc.

compared to the CPI-U and the CPI for college tuition and fees. The CPI-U rose 11.9% between 1991 and 1995, ***while the CPI for tuition and fees rose 37.3%***. Using our weighted sample of four-year colleges, we estimate that tuition and fees rose 36.8% over the sample period—very close to the estimate in the CPI. Adjusting for financial aid, our weighted sample suggests that the net price of college increased by only 28.6% over the sample period for the whole sample. For graduate institutions the net price of college increased by 31% over the sample period, while the increase was only 14.8% for undergraduate institutions.

Quality-adjusting the price indexes leads to further changes in the estimated price index over this time period. The estimates from the quality-adjusted hedonic model for all colleges suggest that the net price of tuition increased by 29.8% from 1991 to 1995. Thus, quality adjusted price indexes show a slightly larger increase than the unadjusted price indexes. One interpretation of this result is that, controlling for the college 'brand' effect, the quality of college services provided are declining. Note that the small difference between the adjusted and unadjusted price index is not driven by the change in any one of the attributes included in the hedonic analysis. Rather it is explained by small changes in a number of the attributes. For example, increases over the five years in pupil-teacher ratios and the percent of minority students have small effects on the estimated price index.

In summary, adjusting for financial aid leads to a 29% decline in the estimated price index, while quality adjusting the results leads to a 4.2% estimated price increase over the sample period. Given both adjustments, our estimate of a price index of college over this time period is 25% below the current price index in the CPI.

VI.   Concluding Remarks

Our analysis indicates that estimating price indexes using hedonic methods is both feasible and useful. Four particular recommendations emerge from this research. First, the price of college should be measured as the 'net' rather than the 'sticker' price for computing a consumer price index. Price indexes computed based upon tuition plus fees net of financial aid indicate significantly lower price rises than the price indexes computed based only upon tuition plus fees. Second, our results indicate that the 'brand' effect of individual colleges is important, so that price indexes should be computed controlling for the college-fixed effect. Third, it is important to include the attributes of colleges in constructing the price index in order to control for changes in the quality of college. And fourth, colleges that have graduate schools demonstrate different pricing than colleges that do not.

While the conceptual framework for implementing a quality-adjusted price index for higher education is straightforward, practical implementation presents empirical challenges – identifying data sources for characteristic variables with consistent definitions, and with consistently available data. An important concern is to construct a representative sample for which data is consistently available over time. Our analysis is based on secondary data provided by the College Board and the Department of Education and contains a significant number of missing values, which introduces the possibility of sample selection bias. Undoubtedly the Bureau of Labor Statistics could assemble a more complete data set for computing price indexes in the future.

References

Abraham, Katharine G., John S. Greenlees, and Brent R. Moulton (1998) "Working to Improve the Consumer Price Index," *Journal of Economic Perspectives* Winter, p. 27-36.

Berndt, Ernst R. (1991) "The Measurement of Quality Change: Constructing an Hedonic Price Index for Computers Using Multiple Regression Methods" Chapter 4 in *The Practice of Econometrics Classic and Contemporary* Addison-Wesley:New York pp. 102-130.

Berndt, Ernst. R. and Griliches, Zvi (1993) "Price Indexes for Microcomputers: An Exploratory Study" in *Price Measurements and Their Uses* Foss, Manser and Young, ed. National Bureau of Economic Research, p. 63-102

Bowen, Howard R. (1980) *The Costs of Higher Education* Jossey-Bass Publishers, San Fransisco.

Bowen, William G. and Derek Bok (1998) *The Shape of the River: Long Term Consequences of Considering Race in University Admissions* Princeton University Press, Princeton, NJ.

Carnegie Foundation for the Advancement of Teaching (1994) *A Classification of Institutions of Higher Education*, 1994 Edition, available at:
http://www.carnegiefoundation.org/OurWork/Classification/CIHE94/classification1994.htm

Clotfelter, Charles T. (1996) *Buying the Best: Cost Escalation in Elite Higher Education* NBER, Princeton University Press, Princeton, NJ

Clotfelter, Charles T. (1999) "The Familiar but Curious Economics of Higher Education" Introduction to a Symposium" *Journal of Economic Perspectives* Winter p. 3-12

Clotfelter, Charles T. and Michael Rothschild (1993) editors *Studies of Supply and Demand in Higher Education* National Bureau of Economic Research, University of Chicago Press, Chicago

Dale, Stacy Berg and Alan B. Krueger (1999) "Estimating the Payoff to Attending a More Selective College: An Application of Selection on Observables and Unobservables" National Bureau of Economic Research Working Paper No. W7322

Griliches, Zvi (1971) editor *Price Indexes and Quality Change: Studies in New Methods of Measurement,* Harvard University Press, Cambridge, MA

Griliches, Zvi, editor (1992) *Output Measurement in the Services Sector* National Bureau of Economic Research, University of Chicago Press, Chicago

Hauptman, Arthur M. with Jamie Merisotis (1990) *The College Tuition Spiral* The American Council on Education and the College Board

Hoxby, Caroline M. (1997) "How the Changing Market Structure of U.S. Higher Education Explains College Tuition," *NBER Working Paper 6323*, December 1997.

Kane, Thomas (1999) *The Price of Admission: Rethinking How Americans Pay for College* Brookings Institution Press, Washington, D.C.

Liegey, Paul R. (1993) "Adjusting Apparel Indexes in the Consumer Price Index for Quality Differences" in *Price Measurements and Their Uses* Foss, Manser and Young, ed. National Bureau of Economic Research p. 209-226.

Manski, Charles F. and David A. Wise (1983) *College Choice in America* Harvard University Press, Cambridge, MA

McPherson, Michael S. and Morton Owen Shapiro (1998) *The Student Aid Game: Meeting Need and Rewarding Talent in American Higher Education* Princeton University Press, Princeton, NJ.

Rosen, Sherwin (1974) "Hedonic Prices and Hedonic Markets: Product Differentiation in Pure Competition," *Journal of Political Economy,* April, pp. 34-55.

Rothschild, Michael and Lawrence White (1993) "The University in the Marketplace: Some Insights and Some Puzzles" *Studies of Supply and Demand in Higher Education* NBER pp.11-37.

Rothschild, Michael and Lawrence White (1996) "The Analytics of the Pricing of Higher Education and Other Services in Which Customers are Inputs," *Journal of Political Economy,* June, pp. 573-586.

Triplett, Jack E. (1971) *The Theory of Hedonic Quality Measurement and Its Use in Price Indexes* BLS Staff Paper 6, United States Government Printing Office, 2901-0634, Washington, DC

Triplett, Jack (1990) "Hedonic Methods in Statistical Agency Environments" in Berndt, E.R. and J.E. Triplett (eds.) *Fifty Years of Economic Measurement: The Jubilee Conference on Research in Income and Wealth,* NBER Studies in Income and Wealth, Chicago: University of Chicago Press.

U.S. Department of Labor, Bureau of Labor Statistics (1997) "How BLS Measures Price Change in the Consumer Price Index for College Tuition and Fixed Fees" BLS Fact Sheet 96-2

Verry, Donald and Bleddyn Davies (1976) *University Costs and Outputs* Elsevier, New York

Winston, Gordon C. (1999) "Subsidies, Hierarchy and Peers: The Awkward Economics of Higher Education" *Journal of Economic Perspectives* Winter p. 13-36.

Appendix I

The following definitions of the categories used in the Carnegie Classifications is taken from: The Carnegie Foundation for the Advancement of Teaching (1994) *A Classification of Institutions of Higher Education*, 1994 Edition, http://www.carnegiefoundation.org/OurWork/Classification/CIHE94/classification1994.htm

Research Universities I: These institutions offer a full range of baccalaureate programs, are committed to graduate education through the doctorate, and give high priority to research. They award 50 or more doctoral degrees1 each year. In addition, they receive annually $40 million or more in federal support.

Research Universities II: These institutions offer a full range of baccalaureate programs, are committed to graduate education through the doctorate, and give high priority to research. They award 50 or more doctoral degrees1 each year. In addition, they receive annually between $15.5 million and $40 million in federal support.

Doctoral Universities I: These institutions offer a full range of baccalaureate programs and are committed to graduate education through the doctorate. They award at least 40 doctoral degrees annually in five or more disciplines.

Doctoral Universities II: These institutions offer a full range of baccalaureate programs and are committed to graduate education through the doctorate. They award annually at least ten doctoral degrees-in three or more disciplines-or 20 or more doctoral degrees in one or more disciplines.

Master's (Comprehensive) Universities and Colleges I: These institutions offer a full range of baccalaureate programs and are committed to graduate education through the master's degree. They award 40 or more master's degrees annually in three or more disciplines.

Master's (Comprehensive) Universities and Colleges II: These institutions offer a full range of baccalaureate programs and are committed to graduate education through the master's degree. They award 20 or more master's degrees annually in one or more disciplines.

Baccalaureate (Liberal Arts) Colleges I: These institutions are primarily undergraduate colleges with major emphasis on baccalaureate degree programs. They award 40 percent or more of their baccalaureate degrees in liberal arts fields and are restrictive in admissions.

Baccalaureate Colleges II: These institutions are primarily undergraduate colleges with major emphasis on baccalaureate degree programs. They award less than 40 percent of their baccalaureate degrees in liberal arts fields or are less restrictive in admissions.

Associate of Arts Colleges: These institutions offer associate of arts certificate or degree programs and, with few exceptions, offer no baccalaureate degrees.

Specialized Institutions: These institutions offer degrees ranging from the bachelor's to the doctorate. At least 50 percent of the degrees awarded by these institutions are in a single discipline.

Specialized institutions include:

Theological seminaries, Bible colleges and other institutions offering degrees in religion: This category includes institutions at which the primary purpose is to offer religious instruction or train members of the clergy.

Medical schools and medical centers: These institutions award most of their professional degrees in medicine. In some instances, their programs include other health professional schools, such as dentistry, pharmacy, or nursing.

Other separate health profession schools: Institutions in this category award most of their degrees in such fields as chiropractic, nursing, pharmacy, or podiatry.

Schools of engineering and technology: The institutions in this category award at least a bachelor's degree in programs limited almost exclusively to technical fields of study.

Schools of business and management: The schools in this category award most of their bachelor's or graduate degrees in business or business-related programs.

Schools of art, music, and design: Institutions in this category award most of their bachelor's or graduate degrees in art, music, design, architecture, or some combination of such fields.

Schools of law: The schools included in this category award most of their degrees in law. The list includes only institutions that are listed as separate campuses in the1994 Higher Education Directory.

Teachers colleges: Institutions in this category award most of their bachelor's or graduate degrees in education or education-related fields.

Other specialized institutions: Institutions in this category include graduate centers, maritime academies, military institutes, and institutions that do not fit any other classification category.

Table 1

Variable Definitions

Variable*	Definition
Tuition + Fees	Undergraduate tuition plus fees
Aid Per Student	Average grants per student
Tuition + Fees - Aid per student	Undergraduate tuition plus fees minus average grants per student
Pupil-Teacher ratio	(# FTE undergrads + grads) / (# FTE Faculty)
% Faculty with PhD	% of faculty with PhD degree
% Part-time Faculty	% of faculty who are part-time
LN Full-time Students	Natural log of the number of full-time undergraduates
LN Part-time Students	Natural log of the numer of part-time undergraduates
PhD granting institution	=1, if institutions grants PhDs; 0 otherwise
NCAA Member	=1, if institution is a member of the National Collegiate Athletic Association
Fraternities and/or Sororities	=1, if institution has fraternity and/or sororities; 0 otherwise
Verbal SAT Score 75th Percentile*	Verbal SAT score of the 75th percentile of entering freshman
Reports SAT Score	=1, if institution reports SAT scores
Requires SATs for Admission	=1, if institution requires SATs for entering freshman
Average Age of Entering Freshman	average age of entering freshman
% Minority Students	% of undergraduates who are racial or ethnic minorities
Weight	Number of FTE undergraduates in 1990-91

* All variables except tuition plus fees comes from the College Board. Tuition and Fees comes from the U.S. Department of Education's Integrated Postsecondary Education Database System (IPEDS)

Table 2

Summary Statistics for 1994-95

	Whole Sample			Graduate Institutions			Undergraduate Institutions		
	Mean	Std. Dev.	Range	Mean	Std. Dev.	Range	Mean	Std. Dev.	Range
Tuition + Fees	7,220	5,388	1612, 26,325	6,190	4,755	1,612, 21,727	13,572	4,679	2,175, 26,325
Aid Per Student	2,619	2,140	339, 10,307	2,180	1,808	463, 9,789	5,325	2,040	339, 10,307
Tuition+Fees-Aid per student	4,601	3,642	0, 20512	4,010	3,275	0, 17,355	8,247	3,679	0, 20,512
Pupil-Teacher ratio	20.366	4.847	6, 55.221	21.051	4.432	8.766, 55.221	16.147	5.174	6, 46.744
% Faculty with PhD	0.787	0.186	.147, 1	0.788	0.187	.292, 1	0.779	0.182	.147, 1
% Part-time Faculty	0.274	0.162	0.017, .903	0.269	0.163	.017, .869	0.309	0.158	.025, .903
LN Full-time Students	8.596	0.998	4.127, 10.200	8.845	0.823	6.333, 10.200	7.063	0.484	4.127, 8.102
LN Part-time Students	6.452	2.009	0, 9.290	6.816	1.821	0, 9.290	4.209	1.626	0, 7.195
PhD granting institution	0.480	0.500	0, 1	0.553	0.498	0, 1	0.033	0.180	0, 1
NCAA Member	0.909	0.288	0, 1	0.944	0.230	0, 1	0.691	0.463	0, 1
Fraternities and/or Sororities	0.847	0.360	0, 1	0.896	0.306	0, 1	0.547	0.499	0, 1
Verbal SAT Score 75th Percentile*	606	46	420, 750	597	46	470, 750	628	54	470, 750
Reports SAT Score	0.736	0.441	0, 1	0.725	0.447	0, 1	0.804	0.398	0, 1
Requires SATs for Admission	0.987	0.112	0, 1	0.991	0.096	0, 1	0.967	0.180	0, 1
Average Age of Entering Freshman	18.578	1.036	17, 32	18.638	1.077	18, 32	18.207	0.620	17, 24
% Minority Students	0.176	0.166	0, 1	0.182	0.168	0, 1	0.137	0.151	.010, .999
N	534			297			237		

Source: 1994-95 College Board Data; 1994-95 IPEDS data.
All variables weighted by FTE in 1990-91.

* Colleges who did not report an SAT score received a value of 0,
and are not included in the mean and standard deviation reported.

Table 3

Means by Year

Whole Sample

Variable	1991	1992	1993	1994	1995
Tuition + Fees	5,480	5,971	6,406	6,810	7,220
Aid Per Student	1,600	1,791	1,998	2,399	2,619
Tuition+Fees - Aid per student	3,880	4,179	4,407	4,412	4,601
Pupil-Teacher ratio	20.643	20.710	20.572	20 270	20.366
% Faculty with PhD	0.806	0.751	0.758	0.766	0.787
% Part-time Faculty	0.272	0.264	0 263	0.268	0.274
LN Full-time Students	8.617	8.620	8 611	8.600	8.596
LN Part-time Students	6.592	6.571	6 607	6.605	6.452
PhD granting institution	0.470	0.458	0.476	0.481	0.480
NCAA Member	0.870	0.882	0 896	0.901	0.909
Fraternities and/or Sororities	0.838	0.837	0 838	0.841	0.847
Verbal SAT Score 75th Percentile*	607	606	605	605	606
Reports SAT Score	0.667	0.693	0 698	0.705	0.736
Requires SATs for Admission	0.987	0.993	0 987	0.987	0.987
Average Age of Entering Freshman	18.628	18.581	18.588	18 530	18.578
% Minority Students	0.145	0.155	0.163	0.170	0.176
N	534				

Graduate Institutions

Variable	1991	1992	1993	1994	1995
Tuition + Fees	4,649	5,097	5,478	5,831	6,190
Aid Per Student	1,329	1,482	1,661	2,003	2,180
Tuition+Fees - Aid per student	3,320	3,615	3,817	3,827	4,010
Pupil-Teacher ratio	21.399	21.470	21.270	20 946	21.051
% Faculty with PhD	0.818	0.751	0.759	0.766	0.788
% Part-time Faculty	0.268	0.258	0 257	0.262	0.269
LN Full-time Students	8.871	8.875	8 864	8.850	8.845
LN Part-time Students	6.979	6.950	6 997	6.999	6.816
PhD granting institution	0.543	0.527	0 548	0.554	0.553
NCAA Member	0.908	0.921	0 934	0.939	0.944
Fraternities and/or Sororities	0.884	0.886	0 886	0.891	0.896
Verbal SAT Score 75th Percentile*	599	598	597	598	597
Reports SAT Score	0.658	0.686	0 688	0.692	0.725
Requires SATs for Admission	0.987	0.995	0 988	0.988	0.991
Average Age of Entering Freshman	18.687	18.631	18.646	18 578	18.638
% Minority Students	0.150	0.159	0.168	0.176	0.182
N	297				

Undergraduate Institutions

Variable	1991	1992	1993	1994	1995
Tuition + Fees	10,600	11,358	12,123	12,848	13,572
Aid Per Student	3,269	3,697	4,077	4,834	5,325
Tuition+Fees - Aid per student	7,331	7,661	8,046	8,014	8,247
Pupil-Teacher ratio	15.981	16.024	16.267	16 096	16.147
% Faculty with PhD	0.730	0.752	0.754	0.763	0.779
% Part-time Faculty	0.297	0.301	0 299	0.306	0.309
LN Full-time Students	7.049	7.044	7 050	7.059	7.063
LN Part-time Students	4.207	4.237	4 207	4.175	4.209
PhD granting institution	0.022	0.030	0 033	0.033	0.033
NCAA Member	0.634	0.645	0 660	0.668	0.691
Fraternities and/or Sororities	0.552	0.541	0 543	0.532	0.547
Verbal SAT Score 75th Percentile*	624	623	624	626	628
Reports SAT Score	0.726	0.735	0.763	0.784	0.804
Requires SATs for Admission	0.987	0.980	0 980	0.976	0.967
Average Age of Entering Freshman	18.264	18.277	18.230	18 232	18.207
% Minority Students	0.118	0.126	0.133	0.134	0.137
N	237				

Source 1991-95 College Board Data 1991-95 IPEDS.
All variables weighted by FTE in 1990-91.

* Mean for colleges who did report an SAT score.

Table 4

Results - Price Equations

	(1) LN(Tuition+Fees)		(2) Weighted** LN(Tuition+Fees)		(3) LN_Net Price*		(4) Weighted** LN_Net Price*	
	Estimate	Std. Error	Estimate	Std. Error	Estimate	Std. Error	Estimate	Std. Error
p92	0.084	0.042	0.103	0.045	0.082	0.047	0.116	0.050
p93	0.155	0.042	0.181	0.045	0.147	0.047	0.186	0.050
p94	0.216	0.042	0.246	0.045	0.155	0.047	0.200	0.050
p95	0.277	0.042	0.313	0.045	0.190	0.047	0.252	0.050
N	2,670		2,670		2,670		2,670	
R**2	0.020		0.022		0.007		0.011	

	(5) LN_Net Price Weighted class dummy		(6) LN_Net Price Weighted graduate		(7) LN_Net Price Weighted undergrad	
	Estimate	Std. Error	Estimate	Std. Error	Estimate	Std. Error
p92	0.121	0.007	0.127	0.010	0.050	0.008
p93	0.195	0.011	0.199	0.014	0.105	0.011
p94	0.214	0.013	0.215	0.017	0.109	0.013
p95	0.270	0.016	0.270	0.020	0.138	0.015
undergrad	-0.033	0.010				
N	2,136		1,188		948	
R**2	0.164		0.171		0.103	

* Net Price equals tuition + fees - aid per student
** Weighted by the number of FTE undergraduates in 1990-91.

Table 5

Results - Hedonic Equation*

	Full Sample		Graduate Institutions		Undergraduate Inst.	
	Estimate	Std. Error	Estimate	Std. Error	Estimate	Std. Error
Undergraduate institution dummy	-0.033	0.010				
p92	0.114	0.008	0.117	0.011	0.052	0.008
p93	0.186	0.011	0.186	0.016	0.105	0.011
p94	0.205	0.015	0.200	0.020	0.103	0.013
p95	0.261	0.017	0.255	0.023	0.132	0.016
Pupil-Teacher ratio	0.005	0.002	0.006	0.003	-0.001	0.001
% Faculty with PhD	0.002	0.010	-0.001	0.014	-0.009	0.044
% Part-time Faculty	-0.066	0.059	-0.082	0.085	0.032	0.053
LN Full-time Students	0.363	0.054	0.329	0.080	0.441	0.042
LN Part-time Students	0.011	0.002	0.013	0.003	0.001	0.003
PhD granting institution	0.024	0.032	0.026	0.042		
NCAA Member	0.037	0.033	0.056	0.050	-0.008	0.025
Fraternities and/or Sororities	-0.054	0.0483	-0.033	0.076	-0.080	0.034
Verbal SAT Score 75th Percentile	0.001	0.000	0.001	0.000	0.000	0.000
Reports SAT Score	-0.132	0.063	-0.183	0.101	-0.073	0.041
Requires SATs for Admission	-0.450	0.142	-0.585	0.207	0.091	0.121
Average Age of Entering Freshman	-0.020	0.006	-0.022	0.008	0.000	0.010
% Minority Students	0.318	0.240	0.426	0.350	-0.102	0.200
N	2,136		1,188		948	
R**2	0.201		0.208		0.208	

* Dependent variable equals LN(Net_price).   Weighted by the number of
FTE undergraduates in 1990-91.

Each regression estimated in first differences.

Table 6

Price Indices

Year	CPI	CPI: College Tuition and Fees	(1) LN(Tuition+Fees)	(2) Weighted LN(Tuition+Fees)	(3) LN_Net Price	(4) Weighted LN_Net Price	(5) Weighted class dummy LN_Net Price	(6) Weighted graduate LN_Net Price	(7) Weighted undergrad LN_Net Price
1991	100.0	100.0	100.0	100.0	100.0	100.0	100.0	100.0	100.0
1992	103.0	110.7	108.8	110.9	108.6	112.3	112.9	113.5	105.2
1993	106.1	121.1	116.8	119.8	115.8	120.4	121.5	122.0	111.0
1994	108.8	129.6	124.1	127.9	116.7	122.2	123.9	124.0	111.5
1995	111.9	137.3	132.0	136.8	120.9	128.6	131.0	131.0	114.8

Year	CPI	CPI: College Tuition and Fees	Adjusted full sample	Adjusted Graduate inst.	Adjusted Undergraduate inst.
1991	100.0	100.0	100.0	100.0	100.0
1992	103.0	110.7	112.1	112.5	105.3
1993	106.1	121.1	120.4	120.4	111.0
1994	108.8	129.6	122.7	122.2	110.9
1995	111.9	137.3	129.8	129.0	114.2